oh no

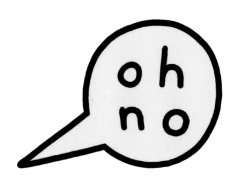

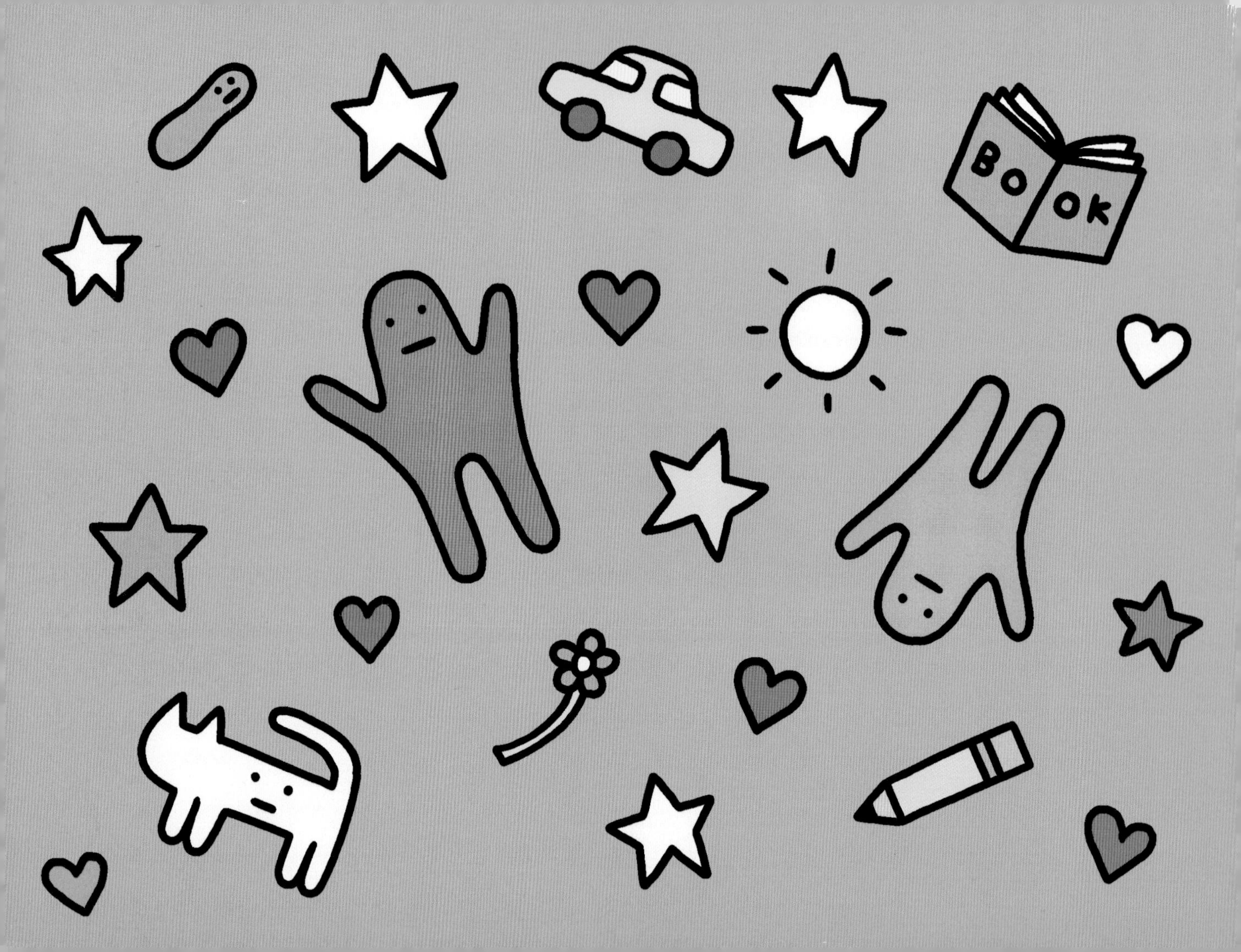
BOOK

oh no

alex norris

Andrews McMeel
PUBLISHING®

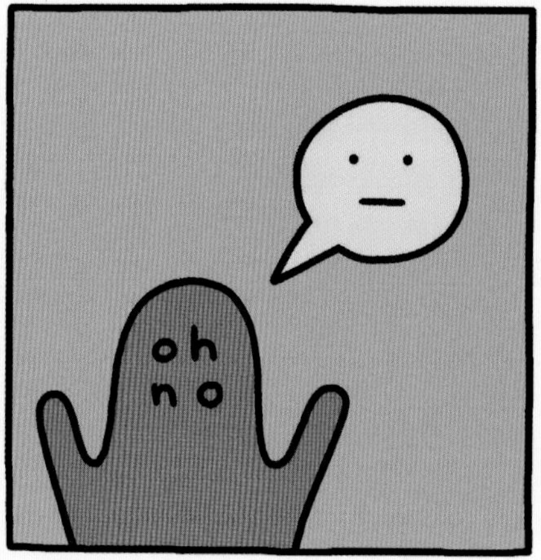
oh
no

CONTENTS

I want to find a particular thing from this book
GITAL ENT
it is a jumble of unindexed comics
oh no
NON-DIGITAL CONTENT

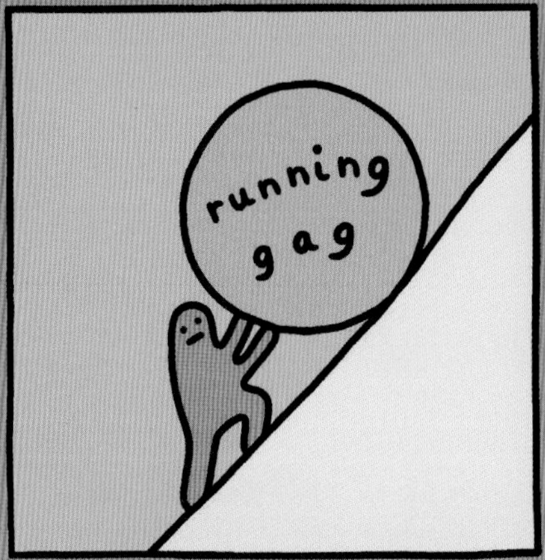
running gag

INTRODUCTION

I do not get you
running gag
I only make sense after being seen multiple times
running gag
not a joke yet
oh no
running gag

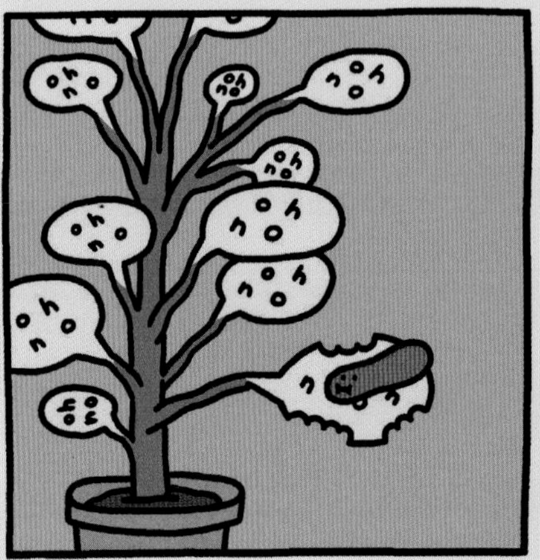
oh no
oh no
oh no
oh no
oh no
oh no
oh no
oh no
oh no

COMICS

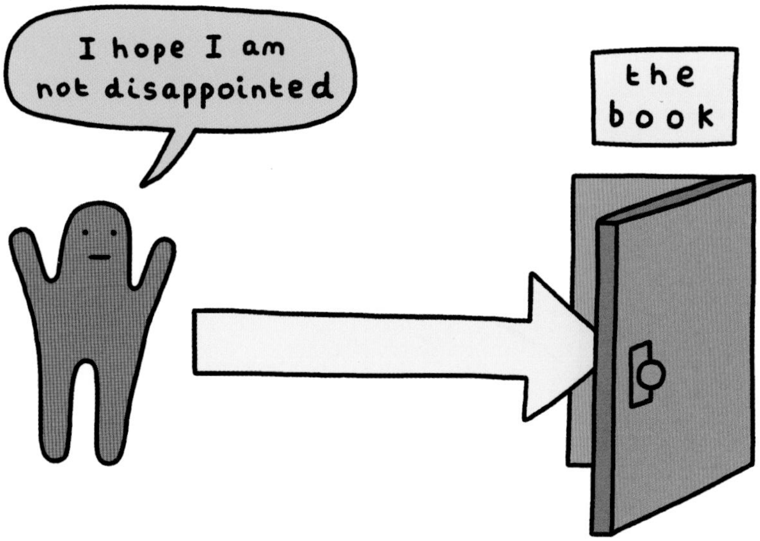
I hope I am not disappointed
the book

PROCRASTINATION

I want to complete a task
BLANK
whoops I did not do it
BLANK
oh no
I am still blank

IMPOSSIBLE

I want to be successful
success
EFFORT
oh no

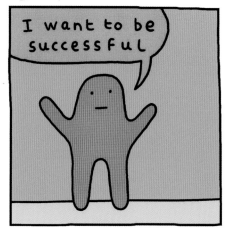

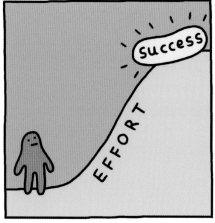

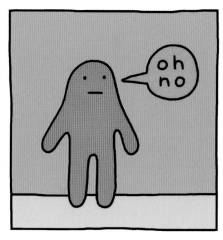

ANSWER

how are you
detailed description of personal tragedies, relationship issues, and financial woes
oh no

VAGITUS

life in the womb is great
everything is soft & straightforward
oh no

LOVE

love is a nice feeling
oh no
stab

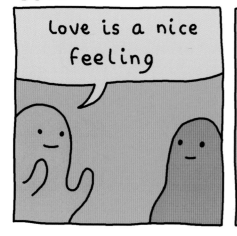

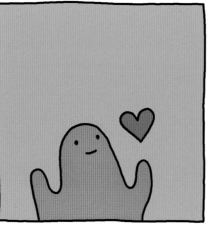

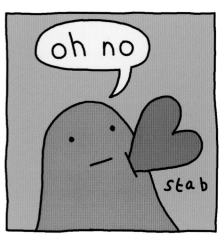

OUTSIDE

I want to go outside
no stay here with me
oh no

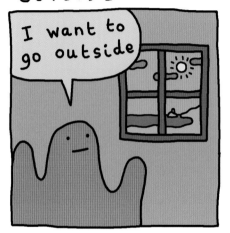

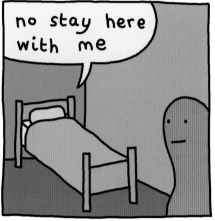

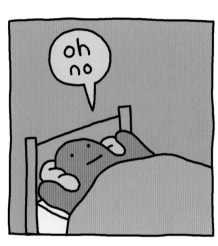

RECIPE

this doesn't look too difficult
RECIPE
food
COOK
COOK
COOK
ingr edie nt
recipe book
COOK
oh no
food

IDENTITY

what do you do?
I am an ARTIST
wow that's amazing
also I work in a supermarket
oh no

BORED

let's play this new board game
game
we need to read the instructions
game
in s tru c tio n s
the inst ructi ons are long & complicated
oh no

GOAL

if I were up there I would be happy
oh no

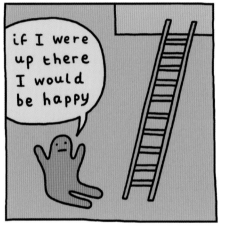

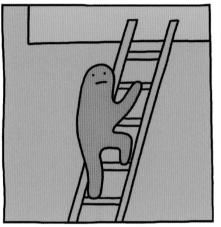

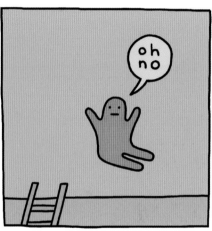

RECIPROCATE

can you do me a favor
yes
LATER
can you do me a favor in return
oh no

VALUE FOR MONEY

this is cheap
cheap thing
expensive thing
expensive thing
so I can buy more of them
cheap thing
cheap thing
cheap thing
cheap thing
cheap thing
you have spent more money overall
oh no
cheap thing
cheap thing
cheap thing
cheap thing
cheap thing
cheap thing

FAMILY

I choose to spend my time with you because I enjoy it
FRIENDS
you will feel obliged to spend time with us
FAMILY
even if we are awful
oh no

TOO SHORT

one haircut please
chop
oh no

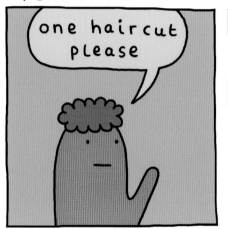

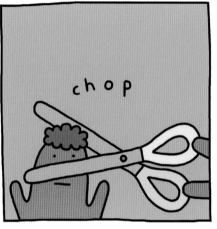

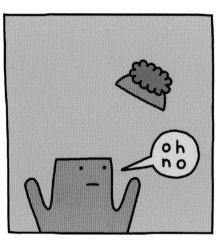

IMAGINATION

oh no

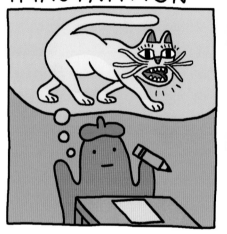

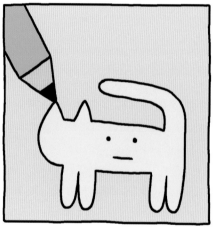

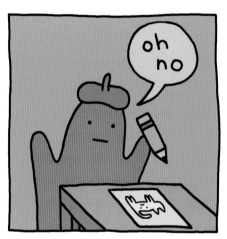

ZOO

I can't wait to go to the zoo to see all the majestic animals
penguin
elephant
sloth
octopus
tiger
ray
crocodile
ant
giraffe
slug
oh no

you should do your bit to help the environment
I am helping
CORPORATION
oh no

HANDS FULL

I would like help
also me
me too
oh no

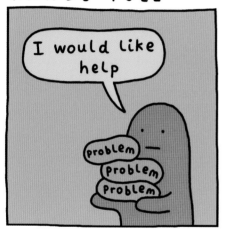

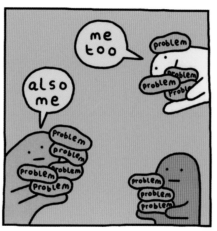

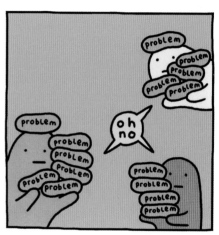

ADAPTATION

BOOK
BOOK:
the
movie
oh no

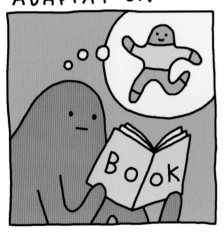

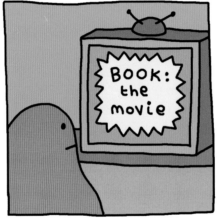

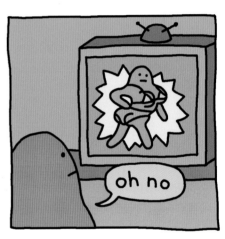

MIRROR MIRROR ON THE WALL

PARODY

you have a bad hat
look at me I am you wearing a bad hat
but now you look the same as me
oh no

HESITATION

OPPORTUNITY
oh look
OPPORTU
I wonder if I should go for it
oh no

FLIRT

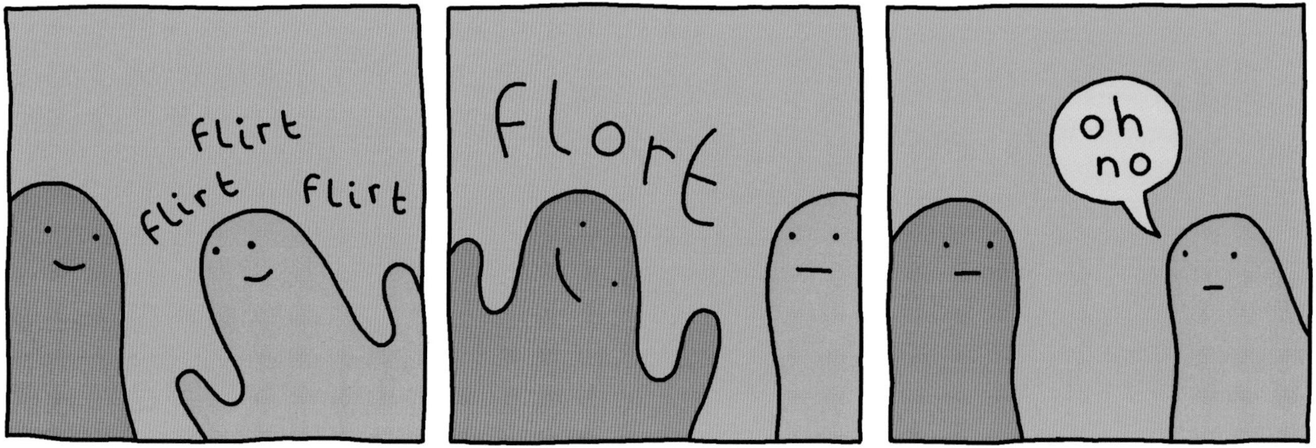
flirt
flirt
flirt
florE
oh no

BUSINESSES ON SOCIAL MEDIA

friendly chatter
funny jokes
heartwarming stories
CORPORATION
oh no

SPECIAL DAY

it is my birth day
AGE
BIGGER EVENT
oh no
AGE

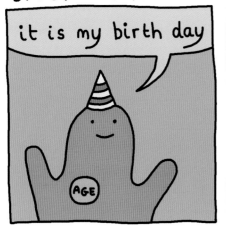

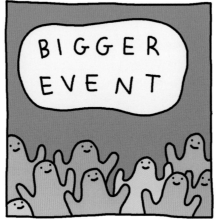

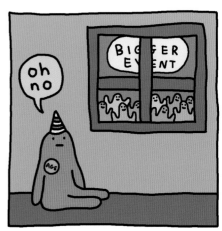

ARM

ZZZZZz

I slept on my arm and it is numb

I do my own thing now

oh no

PRIORITIES

I will help you
their life
help
help
their life
help me
oh no
their life
your life

RESTING SAD FACE

I find it hard to be happy around you
I can't help it, this is my face
oh no
WE ALL DIE

DESECRATION

I have a new sketch book
oh no
ruined

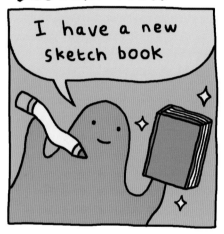

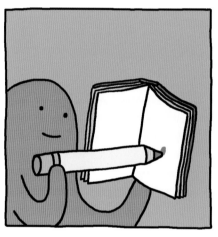

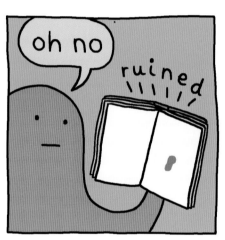

OTHER ARTISTS

Wow this work is amazing
oh and they are much younger than me
ABOUT THE ARTIST
hello
SELF DOUBT
oh no

EXPERIENCE

they say to write from real experiences
DIARY
did nothing
21nd
did nothing
22th
23th
did nothing
24rd
did nothing
25st
oh no

VIOLATED

personal space
oh no

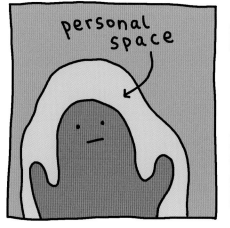

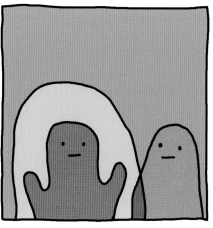

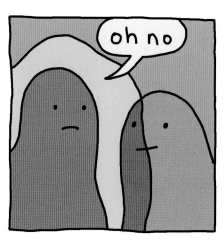

BATTERY

I am a phone, media player, camera, basically your whole life
wow what a technological wonder
oh no
but now I am dead

time to do this work
WORK
DISTRACTION
yay you are finally doing me
WORK
DISTRACTION
oh no
WORK

HEALTHY

I have bought fruit as a healthy snack
oh no

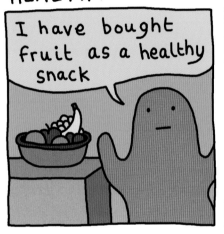

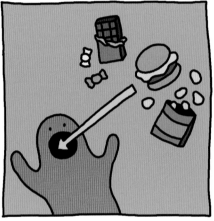

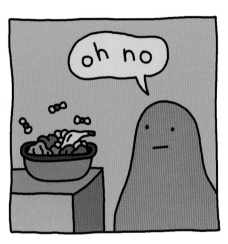

PUBLIC TRANSPORT

BOOK
BOOK
HUMAN BOND CREATED
oh no
BOOK

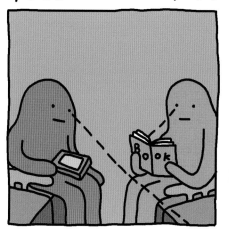

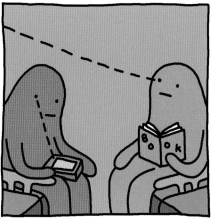

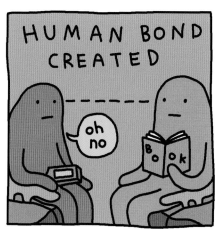

COMPARISON

I have spent years finding my original artistic voice
ART
it reminds me of [another more popular artist]
ART
oh no

BACKFIRE

angry
angry
calm down
angry
angry
angry
oh no

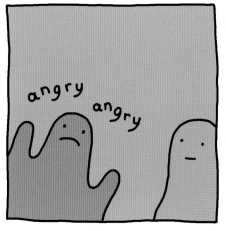

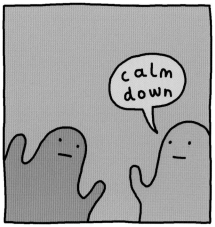

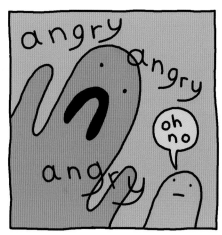

JOB

I do not like being unemployed
BORING
okay here is a job
JOB
BORING
oh no

CLOSE

I like to walk close to my friends
oh no

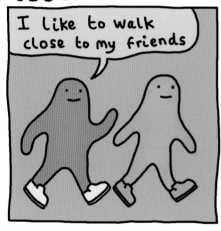

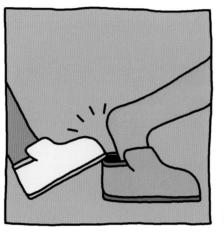

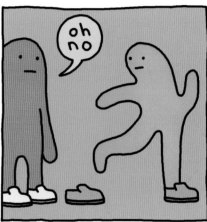

PARENT
I have made an offspring
I will do my best to raise them well
LATER
you messed me up
oh no

PETS

alone
I will befriend this animal with a much shorter life expectancy than me
LATER
alone
oh no
I am dead now

SEQUEL

MOVIE FULL OF INTERESTING NEW IDEAS
I would like to see more of this
SEQUEL FULL OF INTERESTING NEW IDEAS
this is not true to the original
SEQUEL THAT IS A REHASH OF IDEAS FROM THE ORIGINAL
oh no

TINNITUS

I love these sounds
I will listen to them very loudly
now I hear different sounds all the time
oh no
eeeee
eeee

catchphrases are lazy writing
oh no

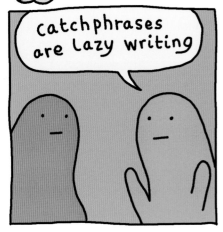

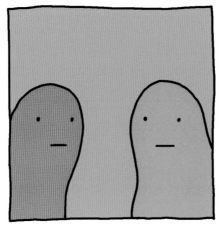

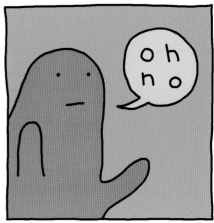

CAT

I am trying to computer
but my cat is in the way
oh no

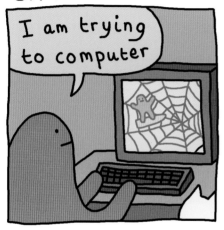

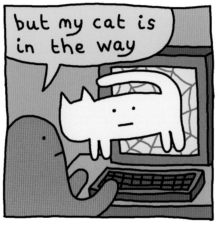

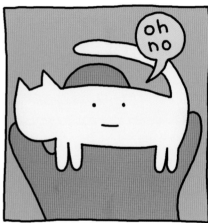

SUBTLE

I will read a satirical cartoon
NEWS PAPER
head line gag
READER
MEANING
METAPHOR
NEWS PAPER
too tiny
oh no
PUNCH LINE

CARTOON GENDER

I must be a man because I am the default
women have extra embellishments
WOMAN
•long hair
•jewelry
•dress
•eyelashes
•lips
•bulging chest
but I also have embellishments
MAN
•short hair
•muscles
•trousers
•hair everywhere
•bulging crotch
you are just a blob
oh no

BEARD

time to shape my facial hair
oh no
BAD

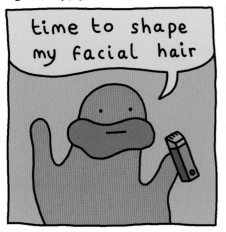

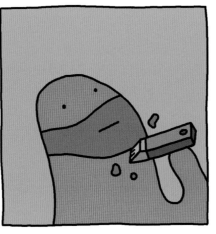

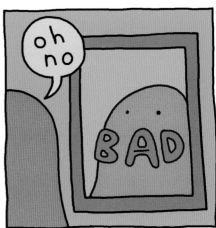

BRA

time to try on new bras
oh no

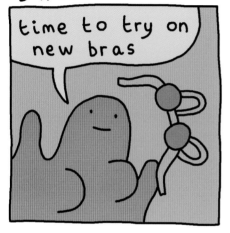

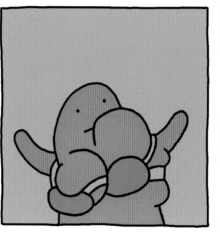

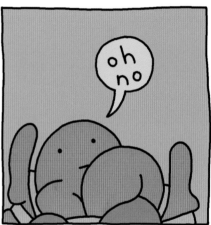

WISH

hello I am a genie
I wish the world were a better place
oh no
R.I.P.

PEER PRESSURE

you are just like my friend
you two will get along
awkward
oh no

AGE

I am not good-looking
oh no
OLD

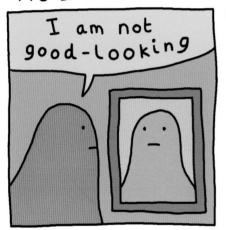

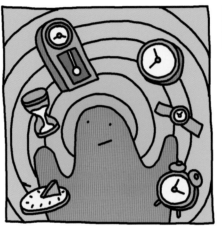

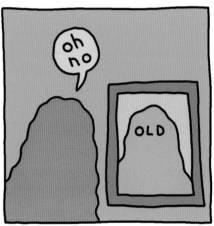

COFFEE
SLEEPY
slurp
COFFEE
TOO MUCH ENERGY
oh no

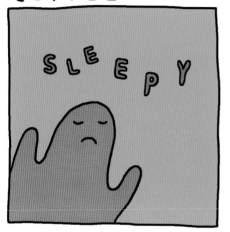

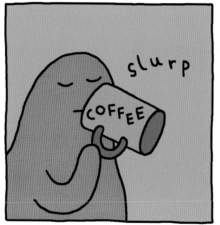

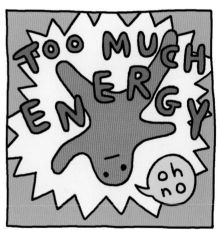

METAPHOR FOR METAPHOR

I am the symbolic representation of the concept of metaphor
METAPHOR
I can describe something as something else
CONFUSION
METAPHOR
so it is easier to understand
oh no
METAPHOR
CONFUSION

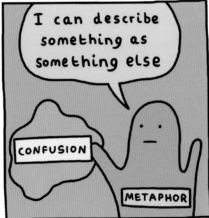

NUANCE

what a complex & nuanced idea
I will fit it into these panels
there are lots of bits left out
oh no

EXAM

I am prepared for this exam
KNOWLEDGE
bye
KNOWLEDGE
oh no

HIGH HEELS

I love my new shoes
I look so sexy
oh no
wobbly walk

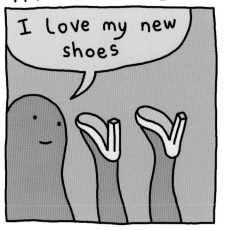

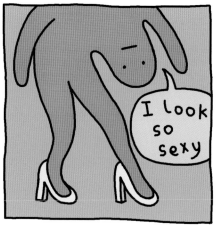

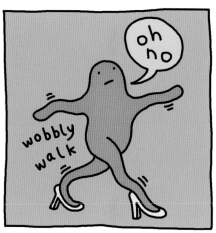

LIFE

I will come for you soon
okay, time to make something of this
oh no

MANSPREAD

I want to sit down on this public transport
but this man is taking up a lot of room
MANLY
oh no

CAR

look at those giant speeding metal things
what stops them from hitting me or each other?
mutual trust
oh no

OFFLINE

I will stop being online
and converse with my friends in person
describing internet content to each other
oh no

SEX

this sex is fun
LATER
oh no

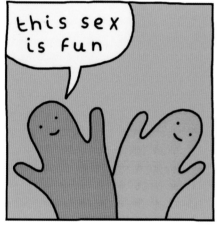

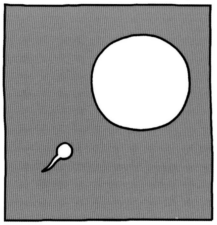

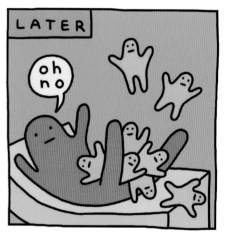

ANYTHING

there are no bound
s
to creativity
I can make art about anything
oh no
running gag

TATTOO

I have put an image on your body forever
NO REGRETS
tattoo
thank you
NO REGRETS
LATER
REGRETS
oh no
NO REGRETS

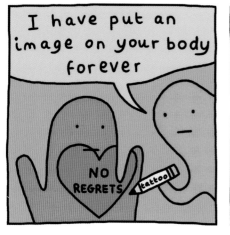

SHAVE

time to make my legs smooth

oh no

ROLLS

I am not too ugly today
time to sit
oh no

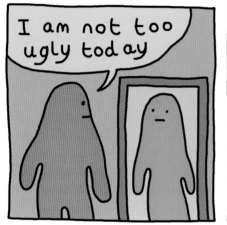

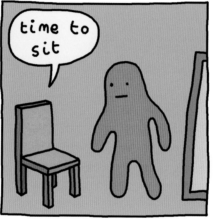

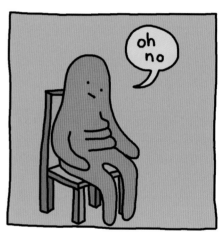

SOCIAL MEDIA

blob
#carefree
52
oh no
WORRY WORRY WORRY WORRY WORRY WORRY WORRY WORRY WORRY

I AM A GOOD COMIC
I AM A GOOD PERSON
it seems like you are a bad person
punch
I AM A GOOD PERSON
look at this sign, not the things I do
oh no
I AM A GOOD PERSON

HUMOR

hahaha
run ning
g a g
what are you laughing at
run ning
g a g
the arrangement of lines & colors on this paper
oh no
co m i cs

HYPOCRISY

I have healed this sick cat back to health
but you are also standing on a cat
you are the worst
oh no

IMITATION

imitation is the sincerest form of flattery

flattery flattery

GLORY

the thing you do

oh no

I'LL

I will do lots of things
illness
oh no

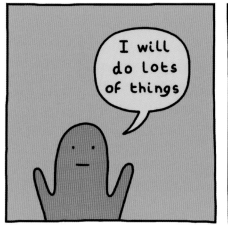

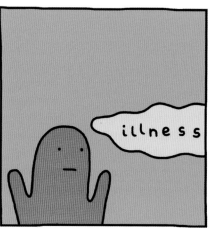

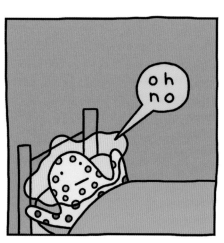

SHOE

shoes are made to protect feet from the floor
but I hope none of the floor gets on my shoe
oh no

RELIGION

be nice to everyone
be nice to everyone
religion
another religion
gi on
oh no
ano rel

VIOLENCE

religion causes violence
rel ig i o n
people are never violent for any other reason
another reason
oh no

NEGATIVE

you are obsessed with finding negativity in everything
but every scenario has uplifting hidden opportunities
but every scenari as uplifting hidde pportunities
oh no

FAD

FAD
FAD
FAD
we are all into this new thing
maybe I will join in
FAD
NEW FAD
NEW FAD
NEW FAD
we are into something else now
FAD
oh no

YOU

I have a book
I will dedicate some of my valuable spare time to reading it
oh no
it is the same joke over & over

I do not like people on their phones all the time
LATER
I will contact a person
they do not respond straight away
oh no

FOIBLE

I love my lover's foibles
foible
foible
foible
foible
foible
foible
foible
THEY ARE ANNOYING NOW
oh no
foible
foible
foible

MEME

I have made a thing
I will take this and frame it in a new way
oh no
BELIEFS YOU DO NOT AGREE WITH

ON REPEAT

what a good song
I will never get tired of this
LATER
oh no

BOOK

can I borrow your book
yes
Book
LATER
thank you for your book
Book
oh no
Book

ANIMALS

this is enter taining
I like this
oh no

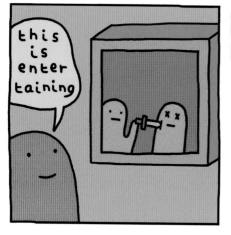

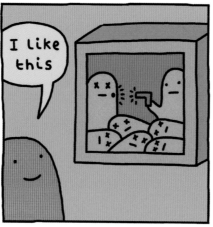

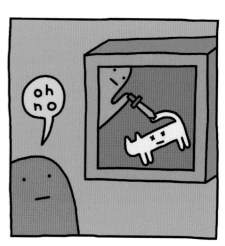

OH NO

NEW

I have a new possession
new thing
I will put it amongst my other possessions
thing
thing
thing
thing
thing
new thing
now we all look crap by comparison
oh no
thing
thing
thing
thing
thing
new thing

PETS ARE WEIRD

we are trying to have lovely sex
sex
sex
but the pet keeps looking at us weirdly
oh no

SADVENTURE

SAD
I should go somewhere new
HOME
NEW PLACE
STILL SAD
oh no

UNIVERSAL

wow this is so universal
oh no
anyone can relate to it
oh no
I do not relate to this
oh no

PLAYBACK

voice
voice
oh no

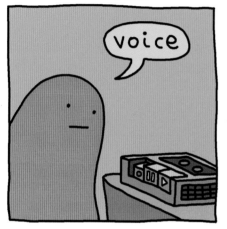

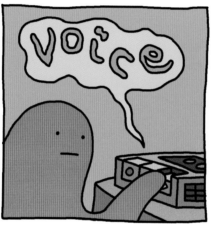

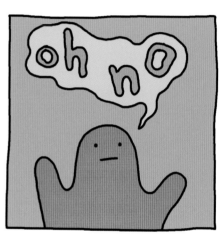

PUBLIC TRANSPORT LOVE

they are so attractive and cool
RUNNING GAG
and they are reading my favorite book ♥
RUNNING GAG
leaves forever
oh no

WHY DIDN'T THEY SAY ANYTHING

I am going to use the toilet and do a quick check of my appearance
o kay
oh no
there was a huge thing on your face the whole time

EDUCATION

here is a brief explanation of sex
LATER
let's do
SEX
oh no
you have no idea what you are doing

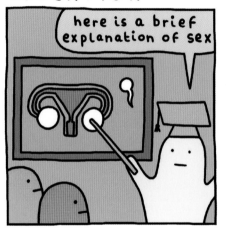

HERO

it is amazing to meet you, I am a big fan
I hope to be a successful artist like you some day
I am sad and I have no money
oh no

SOCIAL INTERACTION

look we are at a party
but I am an introvert
oh no
AWKWARD

CARTOONISTS

cartoonists just create imaginary situations where they win arguments
rather than actually debating their ideas
witty put-down I spent all day writing
oh no

CHALLENGING

but n pro also othi fou says ng nd
oh no
the is u d com psi own ic de
challenging & unusual
I want to read something easy & mind-numbing

VISIONARY

I wonder if my dreams contain prophetic visions of the future
A MUNDANE EVERYDAY SCENARIO
oh no

FIRST DATE

I love cats
me too
now to keep my deep hatred of cats a secret for the rest of this relationship
oh no
I ♥
I ♥

LONG DISTANC
E
let's stay together even though we will be apart
far away
ALL THE NEGATIVES OF BEING IN A RELATIONSHIP
emotional codependence
PLUS ALL THE NEGATIVES OF BEING SINGLE
loneliness
oh no

CUSTOM(IZ)ER

this is an impeccably designed thing with a slick, simple look
I will buy it
money
oh no
and also this decoration

NAIL POLISH

my nail looks nice

chip

oh no

PAY DAY

hooray it is pay day
PAY
BILLS
PAY
oh no

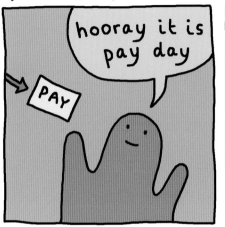

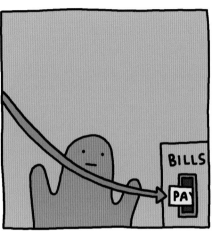

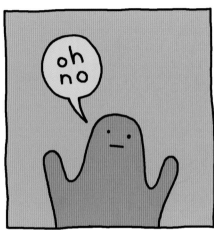

LOVE LIFE

I have crafted a life full of amazing things
let's be in a relation ship
oh no

SPREZZATURA
practice
practice
practice
LATER
wow they are effortlessly good at that
can't do it straight away with no practice
Oh no

NEW YEAR'S EVE

time to have the best night ever
NORMAL AMOUNT OF FUN
oh no

CONVERSATION

conver
sation
haha yes good conversation
oh no

DIFFERENT

I want things to be different
oh no

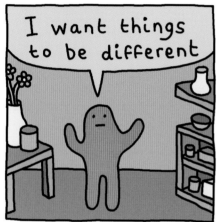

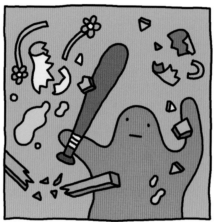

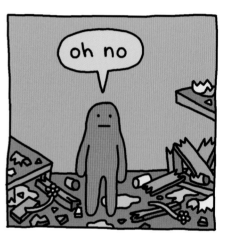

pay attention to me
pay attention to me
pay attention to me
pay attention to me
okay I will pay attention to you
now I do not care
oh no

PEDANT

you and me should have sex
actually it should be: "you and I should have sex"
alone
oh no

ALONE

time to read some relatable content
RELATIONSHIP MEMES
ATTRACTIVE PEOPLE MEMES
oh no

POLITICS

politics is so entertaining
it is like a soap opera
no televisions for pink blobs
oh no

IDEA

look at my idea
ah yes, that is like something I did years ago
oh no
much better

MEMENTO MORI

I am alive
oh no

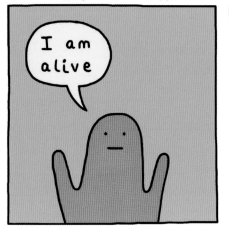

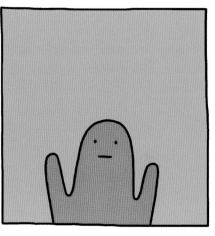

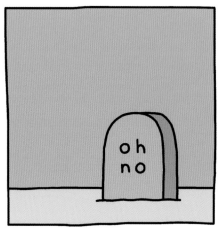

THE END

that is the end of the book
BOOK
oh no

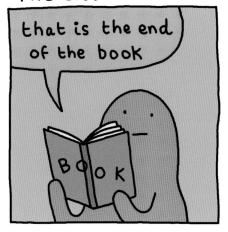

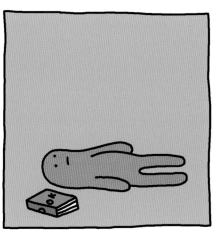

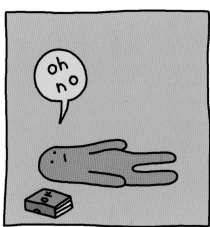

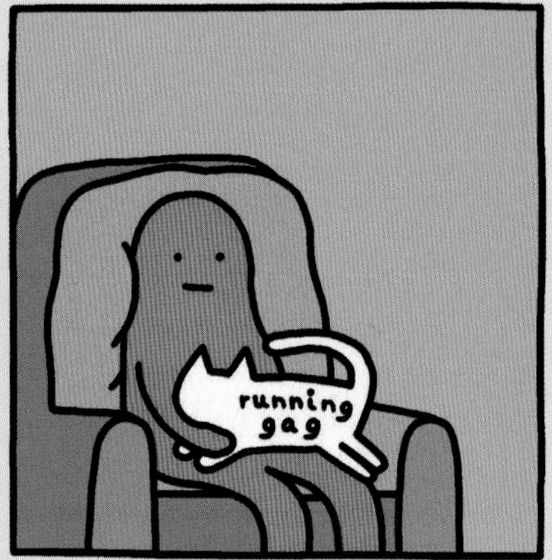
running
gag

ABOUT THE AUTHOR

whoever created me must be a genius
to what magnificent creator does that hand belong
oh no

oh no

Andrews McMeel Publishing
a division of Andrews McMeel Universal
1130 Walnut Street, Kansas City, Missouri 64106

www.andrewsmcmeel.com

19 20 21 22 23 SDB 10 9 8 7 6 5 4 3 2 1
ISBN: 978-1-4494-9253-3
Library of Congress Control Number: 2018959325

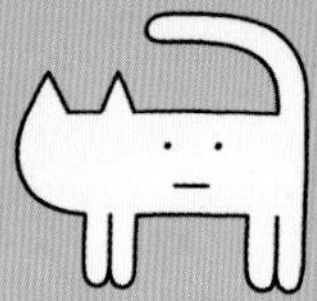

Editor: Allison Adler
Art Director: Diane Marsh
Production Editor: Elizabeth A. Garcia
Production Manager: Tamara Haus

ATTENTION: SCHOOLS AND BUSINESSES
Andrews McMeel books are available at quantity discounts with bulk purchase for educational, business, or sales promotional use. For information, please e-mail the Andrews McMeel Publishing Special Sales Department: specialsales@amuniversal.com.